DETROIT PUBLIC LIBRARY

P9-EFJ-221

DETROIT PUBLIC LIBRARY
CHASE BRANCH LIBRARY
17731 W. Seven Mile
Detroit, MI 48235
935-5346

DATE DUE

MAR 0 3 1999

BC-3

AUG 0 1 1997

CH

NATURE'S MYSTERIES

HOW BEES MAKE HONEY

Michael Chinery

BENCHMARK BOOKS

MARSHALL CAVENDISH
NEW YORK

Benchmark Books
Marshall Cavendish Corporation
99 White Plains Road
Tarrytown, New York 10591-9001

©Marshall Cavendish Corporation, 1997

Series created by The Creative Publishing Company

All rights reserved. No part of this book may be reproduced
or utilized in any form or by any means electronic or mechanical
including photocopying, recording, or by any information storage
and retrieval system, without permission from the copyright holders.

Library of Congress Cataloging-in-Publication Data
Chinery, Michael.
     How bees make honey / Michael Chinery.
         p.   cm. -- (Nature's mysteries)
     Includes bibliographical references (p.   ) and index.
     Summary: Describes the characteristics and behavior of honeybees
and how honey is made and harvested.
     ISBN 0-7614-0453-8 (lb)
     1. Honeybee--Juvenile literature.   2. Honey--Juvenile literature.
  3. Bee culture--Juvenile literature.   [1. Honeybee. 2. Bees.
  3. Honey. 4. Bee culture.]   I. Title. II. Series.
SF523.5.C48 1997   96-19159
595.79'9--dc20   CIP
                                                 AC

Printed and bound in the United States of America

Acknowledgments
Illustrated by Stuart Lafford
The publishers would like to thank the following for their permission to reproduce photographs: cover Gordon
Maclean/Oxford Scientific Films, title page Alastair Shay/Oxford Scientific Films, 4 Kim Taylor/Bruce Coleman, 5 top
G. I. Bernard/Oxford Scientific Films, 5 bottom Ben Osborne/Oxford Scientific Films, 7 top Gordon Maclean/Oxford
Scientific Films, 7 bottom Michael Chinery, 10 Wendy Neefus/Oxford Scientific Films, 12 top D. H. Thompson/Oxford
Scientific Films, 12 bottom Kim Taylor/Bruce Coleman, 13 Scott Camazine/Oxford Scientific Films, 14 Alastair
Shay/Oxford Scientific Films, 15 David Thompson/Oxford Scientific Films, 17 John Cancalosi/Bruce Coleman, 21 David
Thompson/Oxford Scientific Films, 22 top Ronald Sheridan/Ancient Art & Architecture Collection, 22 bottom Jill
Chinery, 23 Mary Evans Picture Library, 24 Dr. Sandro Prato/Bruce Coleman, 25 David Cayless/Oxford Scientific Films,
26 top Treat Davidson/Frank Lane Picture Agency, 26 bottom Francisco Futil/Bruce Coleman, 27 Alain Christof/Oxford
Scientific Films, 28 Gordon Maclean/Oxford Scientific Films, 29 top Peter O'Toole/Oxford Scientific Films, 29 bottom
Gordon Maclean/Oxford Scientific Films

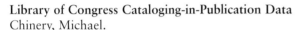

(Cover) A honeybee is covered with grains of pollen while drinking nectar from a flower.

CONTENTS

THE BUSY BEES

Have you ever watched bees buzzing around the flowers in your garden, nearby park, or surrounding countryside? They are busy collecting a sweet sugary liquid called nectar, which they find in the flowers.

After taking it back to their nests, they eat some of the nectar and turn the rest into honey. The bees store the honey in their nests and eat it when there are no flowers for them to visit. Honey is full of sugar and is an excellent source of energy for people as well as for bees.

Bees also collect pollen, the yellow dust produced by the flowers. Look closely and you

This worker honeybee has been busy collecting pollen from flowers. The pollen baskets on its back legs are bulging with the golden powder. The bee will soon have to fly back to its hive to unload the pollen.

Pollen grains are clinging to the hairs all over this bumblebee. The bee combs the pollen from its hair with its middle leg. It then packs the grains into the pollen baskets on its back legs.

There are thousands of different kinds of bees around the world, but the honey that we buy in the store all comes from one particular kind of bee called the honeybee. Millions of these insects live in artificial hives, where they are looked after by beekeepers.

will see the pollen clinging to the bees' hairy coats. Keep watching and you may see a bee combing pollen from its coat. It packs the pollen into pollen baskets on its back legs. The bees take the pollen home and use it as food for themselves and their young.

Collecting pollen and nectar is hard work. A bee visits hundreds of flowers in a day and may work for more than twelve hours a day.

Beekeepers use several different kinds of hives for their bees. The straw one at the front is called a skep.

POLLEN AND NECTAR

Bees get almost all their food from flowers, but flowers don't produce pollen and nectar just so that the bees can eat it; the flowers get something in return. Flowers must produce seeds that can grow into new plants, but a flower cannot produce seeds until it is pollinated. This means that it has to receive pollen from another flower of the same kind. Some flowers rely on the wind to carry their pollen, but most flowers use insects. The bees are the most important of these pollinating insects.

The flowers attract the bees with their sugary nectar, brightly colored petals, and sweet scents. The petals often carry patterns called honey guides. These patterns guide the bees to the nectar and make sure that the insects pick up pollen as well. When the bees enter new flowers, some of this pollen is rubbed off, and seeds can then start to grow.

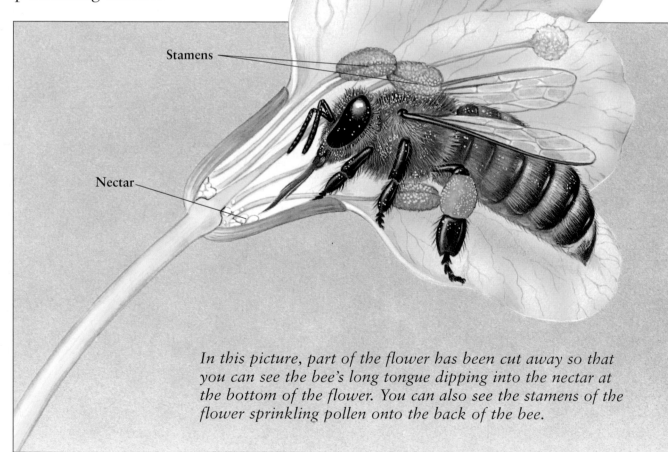

Stamens

Nectar

In this picture, part of the flower has been cut away so that you can see the bee's long tongue dipping into the nectar at the bottom of the flower. You can also see the stamens of the flower sprinkling pollen onto the back of the bee.

▲ *The lines on the petals of this geranium flower guide the bee to the nectar and make sure that it brushes against the stamens to pick up pollen at the same time. Can you see the bee's bulging pollen basket?*

Most flowers produce far more pollen than is needed for pollination so it doesn't matter if the bees eat some of it. You could consider it their reward for carrying the pollen.

Bees and flowers probably appeared on Earth at about the same time — about one hundred million years ago. Since then, the two groups have always been closely linked. Today, there are some really amazing

partnerships between flowers and bees. Some orchids, for example, are pollinated by just one kind of bee, and the bee does not visit any other flowers. No pollen is wasted by being carried to the wrong kind of flower so the orchids can afford to produce more nectar for the bees.

▼ *This strange flower is called a spider orchid, but it looks and smells like a female bumblebee. Male bees are fooled and try to mate with it. They soon give up, but not before they have picked up pollen that they then carry to another orchid.*

THE HONEYBEE

Honeybees live and work together in large colonies. Each colony contains a single queen and up to one hundred thousand other bees. The queen is much bigger than the other bees, and her only job is to lay eggs. All the other bees in the colony are her children, most of whom are female workers. Male bees, called drones, are a little bigger than the workers but don't work at all. Their only job is to mate with queens. There are usually only a few hundred drones in a colony, and they are most common in the spring.

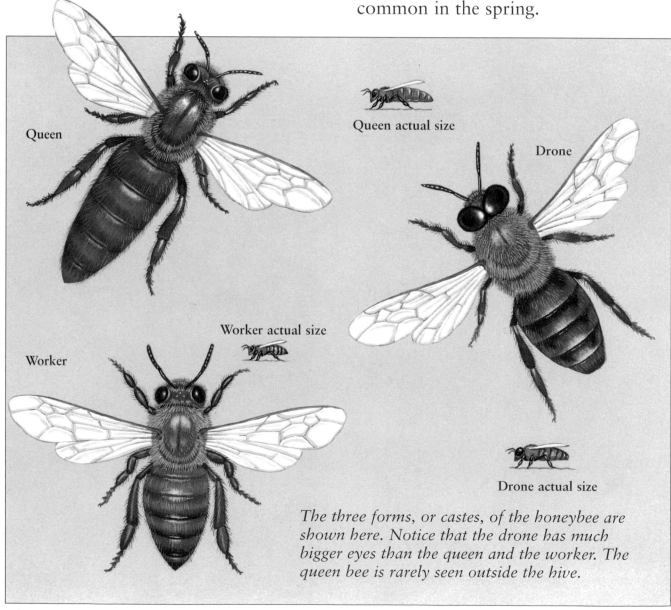

Queen

Queen actual size

Drone

Worker actual size

Worker

Drone actual size

The three forms, or castes, of the honeybee are shown here. Notice that the drone has much bigger eyes than the queen and the worker. The queen bee is rarely seen outside the hive.

Head

Abdomen

Thorax

A bee's legs and wings are all attached to its thorax, the middle part of its body. Stiff hairs form the pollen baskets on its back legs.

Like all insects, the honeybee's body is made up of three parts. The head bears the eyes, feelers, and a long tubular tongue with which the bee sucks nectar from the flowers. The thorax is the middle part of the body; it carries two pairs of wings and three pairs of legs. The abdomen is the last part of the body. It has no legs, but the queen and the workers all have a sting at the end of the abdomen. If a bee is attacked, it pushes out its sting

and injects poison into its attacker. Many bees die after using their stings, but this does not matter if they have helped to drive enemies away and save the colony.

Most parts of the body are covered with hair. The workers' hind legs are fringed with stiff hairs that form the pollen baskets. Since drones and queens don't collect pollen, they have no pollen baskets.

THE HONEYBEE'S HOME

Wild honeybees usually build their nests, often called hives, in hollow trees or other sheltered places. We also use this name for the wooden homes that beekeepers provide for their bees. The nest is made with wax, which the worker bees produce in their own bodies. The wax comes out in little flakes on the underside of the abdomen. By mixing all their wax flakes together, the bees make one or more large sheets called combs. They hang the combs up, side by side. Each comb is covered with neat six-sided wax boxes called cells. There are thousands of these cells in a nest. They are used as nurseries for the young bees as well as for storing honey and pollen.

There are two sizes of cells on the combs. Most of them are about 0.2 inches (0.5 centimeters) across, but larger cells, about 0.25 inches (0.6 centimeters) across, are built around the edges of the combs. The small cells are used for rearing workers, and the larger ones are used as nurseries for the drones.

These honeybees have built their nest in a crack in a tree. You can see the combs and their six-sided cells very clearly.

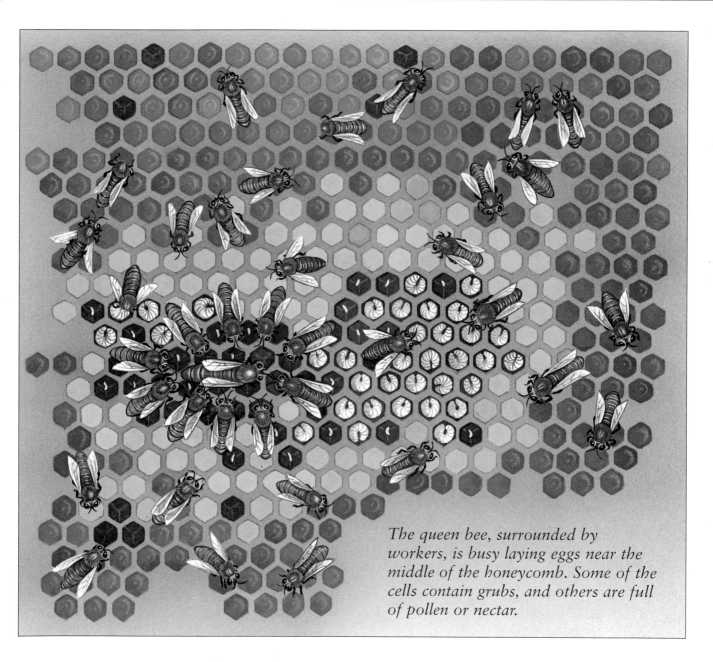

The queen bee, surrounded by workers, is busy laying eggs near the middle of the honeycomb. Some of the cells contain grubs, and others are full of pollen or nectar.

New bees are usually reared in the lower parts of the combs. A cell can be used as a nursery over and over again. The workers clean the used cells carefully, and then the queen lays another egg in each one.

Both kinds of cells are used for storing honey and pollen. Honey is usually stored in the upper parts of the comb, but most of the pollen is stored close to the nursery area. It is used mainly to feed the young bees.

Three days after the queen bee glues an egg in a worker cell, the eggshell melts away and a wormlike white grub appears. The worker bees immediately start to feed it with brood-food, or royal jelly. This is a milky mixture of juices from glands in the workers' mouths. On the third day, the workers start bringing honey and pollen. The grub grows rapidly on this rich food and is fully grown when it is just five days old.

▲ *The wax caps have been removed from these cells to show the heads of the pupae inside them. The eyes and feelers of the young bees are already well-developed, but you can see that they have no hair yet.*

New worker emerging

Right in the center of this picture you can see a new worker struggling out of its cell. The pale bee to its right has just left its cell and will soon get darker. Other workers are cleaning up the surrounding cells.

At this point, the grub stops eating, and the workers cover the cell with wax. The grub turns first into a pupa and then into an adult bee. About ten days later, the new bee bites its way out of its cell and sets to work almost at once.

For the first four or five days, the new bees work as housemaids. They clean out the cells in which they grew up and then turn to feeding the grubs and the queen. When they are about two weeks old, the bees become builders and start making new cells. At about this time, they also start to handle the pollen and nectar brought back by the collectors and begin to change the nectar into honey. When the bees are about three weeks old, they are ready to go out and collect food themselves.

Most honeybee workers live for only a few weeks, but those that grow up late in the summer survive until the spring. They stay in the nest all through the winter and feed on stored honey. Queen bees usually live for about three years.

The bee on the left is receiving food. Adult bees are always sharing food with each other; this helps to keep them all friendly and ensures that they all work together for the good of the colony.

GATHERING FOOD

Worker bees do not go out every day. They stay at home and feed on stored honey when the weather is bad and when there are no suitable flowers for them to visit.

But when they do go out, they work very hard, sometimes flying two or three miles (three to five kilometers) from their nests to collect food. They make several journeys in a day, visiting hundreds of flowers on each journey. They have a very good sense of direction and can recognize and remember landmarks very well. So they have no trouble in finding their way back to the nest.

Pollen is usually collected by the younger workers who have only just started to go out and collect food. Older workers usually collect nectar. A bee generally keeps to one kind of flower on each journey. This is good for the flowers because their pollen is not wasted by being taken to the wrong kinds of flowers. Food-gathering bees are called foragers.

Pollen is carried home in the pollen baskets on the bees' back legs. In the hive, the pollen is unloaded into the cells. Housemaid bees mix it with saliva and a little honey to stop it from going rotten.

This worker bee is plunging its tongue into a flowerhead to suck up the sweet nectar. Bees make many foraging journeys each day, visiting hundreds of flowers on each journey.

These housemaids are busy packing pollen into the comb. Some cells near the top have already been covered with wax.

Then, they pack the pollen tightly into the cells and cover it with wax. Most of this pollen is fed to the grubs.

The sugary nectar is carried in the bee's honey stomach. A full load fills nearly half of the abdomen. The foragers bring up the nectar when they get home, and the household bees line up to take it from them. Some nectar may be given to the grubs immediately, but most of it is taken away to be turned into honey.

This drawing of the inside of a worker bee shows the honey stomach full of nectar. The abdomen has to stretch to hold it.

Honey stomach

MAKING HONEY

The nectar brought back by foraging bees contains a lot of water, which must be removed before the honey can be made. When one of the household bees takes a load of nectar from a returning forager, it goes to a quiet part of the nest and starts to roll the nectar around in its mouth. The warmth drives some of the water off, and after about twenty minutes, the bee tips the nectar into a cell. The household bees also help the nectar to dry by fanning the cells with their wings.

This worker bee is holding her tongue out, ready to receive a load of nectar that has been collected by a forager.

After rolling the nectar around in her mouth for a while, the worker bee tips it into a cell. The nectar is already starting to turn into honey. Many loads of nectar are needed to fill each cell.

While the nectar is drying, the sugars in it are also changing. These changes begin as soon as the nectar is swallowed by the foraging bees, and are caused by the bees' saliva and other juices. The process continues while the nectar is being rolled around in the jaws of the household bees, and it is completed in the cells. Most of the water disappears after about five days, and the nectar changes into sticky honey that is nearly all sugar. The bees then cover the cells with wax and leave the honey until it is needed.

The bee on the left is fanning her wings over the cells. This helps to dry the nectar — just as wet clothes on the line dry better on a windy day.

When the cell is full, the worker bees cover it with wax, which they shape with their jaws.

Each worker eats about 0.004 of an ounce (0.125 grams) of honey — equal to about half the weight of a corn kernel — while it is a grub and a lot more while it is an adult. So you can see that a colony with one hundred thousand bees needs to produce a lot of honey. Bee experts have worked out that a large colony needs to produce about 175 pounds (80 kilograms) of honey every year.

The sugar in the honey prevents it from going bad. It also gives the bees a lot of energy. The bees make sure that they take a supply when they go out to forage.

17

DANCING FOR DIRECTION

When a worker bee finds a good source of food, she has a wonderful way of telling the other bees about it. She goes back to the nest and dances on the combs.

If the food is quite close to the nest, the bee performs the round dance. She goes round and round, first one way and then the other. The other bees get very excited and follow her. They pick up the scent of the flowers she has been visiting and then fly off to find the flowers themselves.

If the food is more than about three hundred feet (one hundred meters) away, the returning bee performs the waggle dance. This tells the other bees the direction of the food and also how far they must fly to find it. The waggle dance is shaped a bit like an 8, and while the bee runs along the middle bit, she waggles her abdomen. If the food is in the same direction as the sun, the central run of the dance is straight up the comb. If the food is to the left or right of the sun, the bee alters the direction of her dance by the correct amount to the left or right of the upright line. The other bees follow her in the dance and remember the direction when they fly out to find the food.

The distance of the food is given by the speed of the waggle dance. If the food is about 450 feet (150 meters) away, the bee does

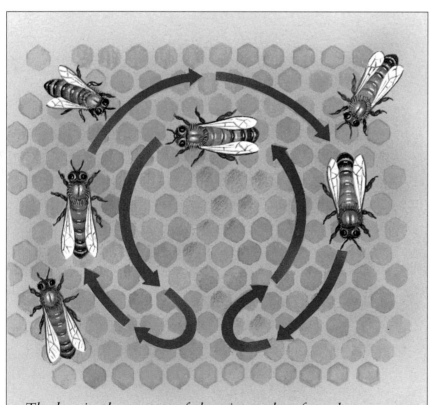

The bee in the center of the picture has found some flowers full of good nectar, and she is performing the round dance on the honeycomb. Other bees are getting excited and are beginning to follow her. They will soon fly out to find the flowers themselves.

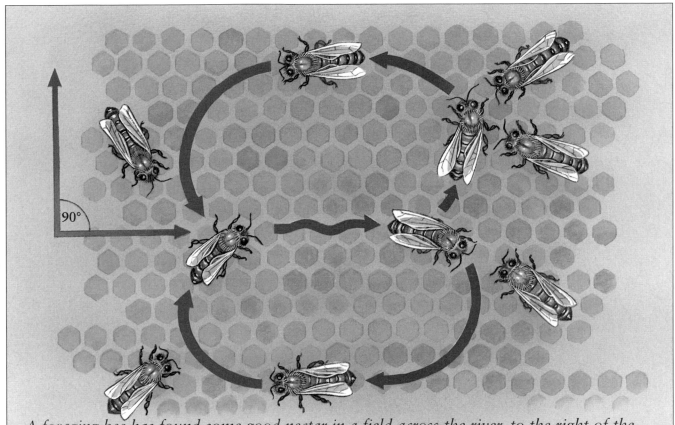

A foraging bee has found some good nectar in a field across the river, to the right of the sun. When she comes back to the hive, she performs the waggle dance (above). The central run of the dance goes to the right; this tells the other bees that they must fly to the right of the sun when they go out to collect the nectar.

a complete circuit in about two seconds, but if it is three miles (five kilometers) away, she takes seven or eight seconds for each circuit.

Bees also have a wonderful sense of time. They seem to know how long they spend away from the nest and allow for the change in the sun's position to find their way home.

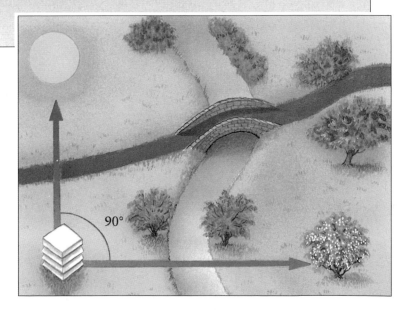

SWARMING FROM THE NEST

The queen honeybee lays hundreds of eggs every day in spring and summer. Though lots of workers die every day as well, the nest soon gets overcrowded. It is then time for some of the bees to leave and look for a new home. A few thousand workers fill themselves with honey and stream out of the nest in a swarm, with the queen in the middle. With thousands of wings whirring at the same time, they make quite a lot of noise.

The swarm settles after a while, often in a tree. The swarm is very heavy, and its weight sometimes snaps the branches. The bees form a tight bunch, with the queen right in the middle. Some of the workers then fly off to find a place for a new nest.

A swarm leaving the hive can contain thousands of bees, often about half of the original population of the hive. The queen is somewhere in the middle of the swarm. Some of the workers have already decided where the swarm will land and, by leaving a trail of scent, they guide it to the chosen spot — often on the branch of a tree.

The worker bees generally start to make new queen cells before a swarm leaves. You can see a queen cell here. It is much bigger than the normal cells. The first new queen to leave her cell usually breaks open all the other queen cells and kills the pupae. She then has no rivals, and she takes over the colony.

A bee that finds a suitable place comes back and dances on the surface of the swarm. The dance is like that of the food-collectors and encourages other bees to go and have a look at the site. If enough of them are happy with it, the whole swarm flies off to start building the new nest.

When a swarm leaves a nest, the workers left behind have to rear a new queen. They enlarge some cells at the edge of the comb and feed the grubs in them entirely on royal jelly. These grubs grow into new queens, and one of them takes over as ruler of the colony. But before she can lay any eggs, she must fly out and mate with some drones.

The bees swarm mainly in late spring. Beekeepers try to gather the swarms and put them into artificial hives, where the bees usually settle down and build their nests.

21

HONEY IN HISTORY

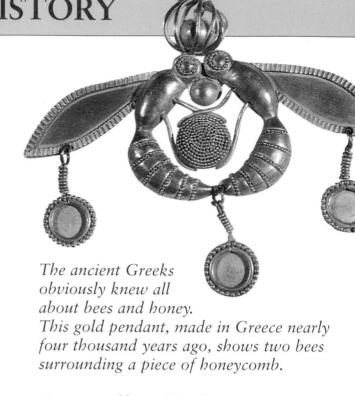

Paintings on the walls of caves in Spain and other places show people collecting honey from bees' nests. These paintings are at least ten thousand years old so we know that people have been using honey for a very long time. Sugar was not widely used until about five hundred years ago; until then, honey was used to sweeten food. It was also used in medicines and for making alcoholic drinks. Some people thought it was a magical substance and used it in religious ceremonies. Honey was very precious and valuable stuff. In the sixteenth century, a gallon (4.5 liters) of English honey was worth six geese.

The ancient Greeks obviously knew all about bees and honey. This gold pendant, made in Greece nearly four thousand years ago, shows two bees surrounding a piece of honeycomb.

Carvings of bees, like this one on a pillar at the Temple of Karnak, decorate many ancient Egyptian buildings.

This two hundred-year-old picture shows the wide range of hives in use at that time. The two people on the right are trying to knock a swarm from a branch into a box.

Honey was originally collected by people breaking into wild bees' nests. This still happens in some places, but most of our honey now comes from artificial hives. Carvings and paintings in Egyptian tombs and temples show that bees were being kept in hives at least five thousand years ago. The ancient Egyptians stored large quantities of honey in their temples as gifts to their gods, and Egypt was often called the land of the bee.

Straw, clay pots, and wood have all been used to make artificial hives. The bees don't mind what the hives are made of as long as they are warm and dry. Before taking honey from the hives, the earliest beekeepers probably killed most of their bees by filling the hives with smoke or by plunging the hives into water. They ate the wax combs and pollen with the honey — and probably a lot of dead bee grubs as well! Some people still like to eat their honey in its waxy combs, but modern beekeeping systems ensure that the honeycombs do not contain any bee grubs!

HONEY TODAY

Modern beehives consist of wooden sections stacked on top of each other. The beekeeper hangs several wooden frames in each section. The frames are like picture frames, but instead of containing glass, each one has a sheet of thin wax inside. The bees build their combs on this ready-made foundation. It saves them time and effort so they can get on with making honey more quickly.

This hive has been opened to show the frames on which the bees build their combs. Beekeepers wear special clothing to stop them from getting stung.

Honey is stored in the combs in the upper parts of the hive, which are separated from the rest by a sheet of metal called a queen excluder. This has holes big enough for the workers to get through but too small for the queen so the honeycombs never contain any eggs or grubs.

When the bees have filled the combs with honey and covered them with wax caps, the beekeeper takes the combs away. Sugar is given to the bees to replace the honey, otherwise the bees would not have enough food for the winter.

The wax caps are removed, and the combs go into a machine like a clothes dryer. The honey flies out of the combs and collects at the bottom of the machine. It is then put into jars ready to be sold in stores. The wax from the combs is used to make candles and polish, as well as new foundations for the frames.

Do you like runny honey or set honey? All honey is quite runny at first, but it normally starts to set or

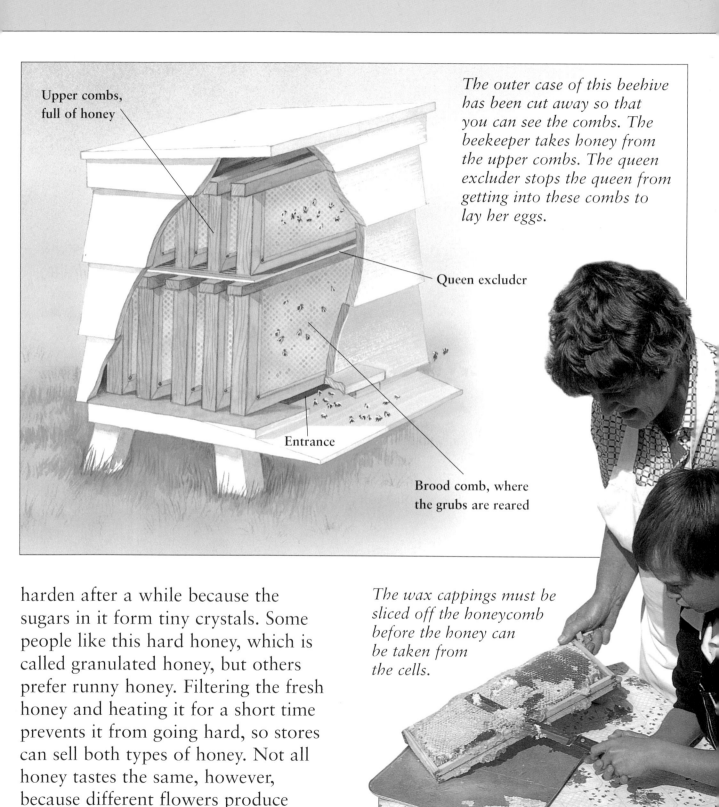

Upper combs,
full of honey

The outer case of this beehive has been cut away so that you can see the combs. The beekeeper takes honey from the upper combs. The queen excluder stops the queen from getting into these combs to lay her eggs.

Queen excluder

Entrance

Brood comb, where
the grubs are reared

The wax cappings must be sliced off the honeycomb before the honey can be taken from the cells.

harden after a while because the sugars in it form tiny crystals. Some people like this hard honey, which is called granulated honey, but others prefer runny honey. Filtering the fresh honey and heating it for a short time prevents it from going hard, so stores can sell both types of honey. Not all honey tastes the same, however, because different flowers produce different flavors.

BEE-WARE!

Although they give painful stings, honeybees have plenty of enemies. Bears love honey and break into the bees' nests to steal it whenever they can. The bees get very angry and sting the bears, but the bears don't seem to mind too much. Their thick coats give them a lot of protection. As well as breaking into wild bees' nests, bears sometimes wreck beekeepers' hives and take away sections to eat the honey later.

▲ *This American black bear has knocked over a wooden beehive and is about to pull out the combs and have a feast of honey, despite the angry bees.*

Badgers also like to steal honey from bees' nests. The African honey badger, or ratel, often teams up with a little bird, called a honeyguide, that feeds on wax and bee grubs. The bird makes a lot of noise when it sees a ratel

An African ratel, or honey badger, has dragged a comb from a wild bees' nest and is eagerly lapping up the honey oozing from the cells.

by the poison in the stings, but they sometimes discharge the stings by hitting the insects on hard objects before swallowing them.

The bee-killer wasp catches honey bees, paralyzes them with its sting, and carries them to its burrow, where the wasp's grubs feed on the paralyzed bees. Bee-killer wasps are so common in some parts of Europe that beekeeping is almost impossible. Tiny spiderlike creatures called mites also attack bees and can kill whole colonies if they get into the hives.

This European bee-eater has caught a bumblebee. It may knock out the sting before swallowing the insect. Because no bees fly around in cold weather, the bee-eater has to fly south to Africa for the winter.

or other large animal, and the animal then follows the bird. When the honeyguide finds a bees' nest, the ratel breaks into it and eats the honey and the grubs. The honeyguide later feeds on the wax combs and any remaining grubs. People also sometimes follow the honeyguide to get a good supply of honey.

In some warm countries, honeybees are eaten by colorful birds called bee-eaters. These birds catch the bees in midair. They are probably unaffected

OTHER KINDS OF BEES

Bumblebees are bigger than honeybees and much hairier. There are many different kinds with various color patterns, and most of them live in the cooler parts of the world. Bumblebee colonies generally contain only a few hundred bees. Unlike the honeybees, their colonies last for just a few months, and all the bees except the queens die at the end of summer.

The queen bumblebee sleeps through the winter and builds her nest in the spring — but not before she has built up her strength by feeding on pollen and nectar from the spring flowers. Most bumblebees make their nests on or under the ground, often in old mouse holes. The nest is a ball of dry grass and moss with a cushion of pollen in the middle. The queen also makes a thimblelike honey pot and fills it with nectar for use in bad weather. Some of the water is removed from the nectar, but it is not converted into real honey.

Bumblebees, like honeybees, are very good at finding their way back to their nests. They use the sun and also remember landmarks to guide them to the nest entrances.

Whether they live in colonies or on their own, the story of bees is a fascinating one. But it is the honeybees in their huge colonies that are perhaps the most fascinating of all. Only honeybees provide us with that most delicious of foods — honey.

▼ *Solitary bees, such as this mining bee, are very important pollinators of apple and other fruit trees. They carry the pollen on their legs or under their abdomen. Many of them build their nests in the ground, which is why we call them mining bees.*

▲ *The yellowish balls in this bumblebee nest are cocoons containing pupae. Old cocoons are used for storing nectar. You can see some shiny nectar near the middle of the picture.*

Not all bees live in colonies like the honeybees and bumblebees. Most bees live alone. They are called solitary bees. Each female makes her own nest and lays her eggs in it. She fills it with pollen and nectar for her grubs to eat, and then she flies away. She never sees her babies.

GLOSSARY

colony: a group of animals living together.

feeler: one of two slender stalks on the bee's head used to pick up scents and feel its way around.

forager: a food collector.

gland: a part of the body making and releasing particular substances, such as wax or royal jelly.

grub: the second stage in a bee's life, after it has hatched from the egg but before it becomes a pupa.

honeycomb: a wax comb full of honey.

paralyzed: unable to move.

pupa: the third stage in a bee's life, during which the grub's body changes into that of an adult.

royal jelly: the rich food made in the workers' bodies and fed to the grubs. It is also called bee-milk and brood-food.

stamen: the part of a flower that carries its pollen.

FURTHER READING

Crewe, Sabrina. *The Bee*. Chatham, NJ: Raintree Steck-Vaughn Publications, 1997.

Fischer-Nagel, Andreas, and Heiderose Fischer-Nagel. *Life of the Honeybee*. Minneapolis, MN: Carolrhoda Books, 1986.

Harrison, Virginia. *The World of Honeybees*. Milwaukee, WI: Gareth Stevens, Inc., 1989.

Harwood, Lynne. *Honeybees at Home*. Gardiner, ME: Tilbury House Publications, 1994.

Hogan, Paula Z. *The Honeybee*. Chatham, NJ: Raintree Steck-Vaughn Publications, 1984.

Otani, Takeshi. *The Honeybee*. Chatham, NJ: Raintree Steck-Vaughn Publications, 1986.

Parramon, Y. M. *The Fascinating World of Bees*. Hauppauge, NY: Barron's Educational Series, Inc., 1991.

INDEX

Numbers in *italic* indicate pictures